LANGSTON

Written by
Michael G. Grindstaff

Illustrated by
Tracy Grindstaff

To my beautiful daughters, Amberlin and Isla.
May your imagination grow with each day.

Langston
Written by Michael G. Grindstaff
Illustrated by Tracy Grindstaff
Book Design by Tara Sizemore
Published December 2021
Skippy Creek
Imprint of Jan-Carol Publishing, Inc

This is a work of fiction. Any resemblance to actual persons, either living or dead is entirely coincidental. All names, characters, and events are the product of the author's imagination.

This book may not be reproduced in whole or part, in any manner whatsoever without written permission, with the exception of brief quotations within book reviews or articles.

Copyright © Michael G. Grindstaff
ISBN: 978-1-954978-33-1
Library of Congress Control Number: 2021951617

You may contact the publisher:
Jan-Carol Publishing, Inc.
PO Box 701
Johnson City, TN 37605
publisher@jancarolpublishing.com
www.jancarolpublishing.com

Author's Note:

Thank you to all that have supported this project by giving inspiration, prayer, and finances. I could not have done this without you all. This is for you!

There was a young boy named Neil who had a friend.

Langston was the friend's name.

They would play all day and have fun with no end.

Sometimes at night young Neil would awake.

Langston would urge him.

So, Neil and Langston would stuff their faces with cake.

Neil AND Langston

had all sorts of adventures.

They flew!

They fought giants!

They stole Papaw Clark's dentures.

As the years rolled by, they became the best of pals!

They laughed!

They cried!

Neil and Langston even talked about snotty-nosed gals.

Wherever Neil went, he brought Langston along.

At baseball practice and piano lessons...

Even at school where Langston didn't stay long.

When Neil felt he needed a friend to be near, he would think of Langston.

And the joyful Langston would appear!

As time passed by, and Neil grew in age...

his relationship with Langston began to change.

Neil went to middle school.

He went to high school, then to college, and then life!

After many years,
Neil found himself a wife.

Sometimes Neil felt he needed a friend to be near,
but he never thought of Langston
for years upon years.

Time went on as it always does.
Neil and his wife had a daughter whom they loved.

They named her Belle, and she grew to be kind.
She loved to play and to use her mind.

One day Belle ran to her father
with excitement and glee!

"Daddy, come see! Daddy, come see!
Meet my friend out by the tree!"

Neil replied, "A friend? What friend?
Next to the tree you say?
I didn't know you had anyone over to play."

"I didn't, Daddy! I just met him today!"

Reaching the tree, Neil was caught with surprise.

There was Langston looking into his eyes!

Neil had not seen Langston for years.
He ran to Langston with joyful tears!

It was the greatest day Neil had experienced in some time,
he was with Belle and Langston,
and he knew everything would be just fine.

CPSIA information can be obtained
at www.ICGtesting.com
Printed in the USA
BVHW020227040122
625375BV00016B/391